Kekekabic

poems by

Eric Chandler

Finishing Line Press
Georgetown, Kentucky

Kekekabic

ACKNOWLEDGMENTS

Thank you to Sharon Harris and The Jackpine Writers' Bloc for previously publishing "20180722" in *The Talking Stick* (Vol. 28) in September, 2019.

Thank you to Ben Wilkinson, Kim Moore, and Paul Deaton for previously publishing "20180611" in the anthology *The Result Is What You See Today: Poems About Running* (The Poetry Business, 2019).

Thank you to Abby E. Murray and *Collateral Journal* for previously publishing these four haibun (20180330, 20180606, 20180610, and 20181001) as "Can't Outrun It" in Issue 4.1 in November, 2019.

Thank you to Ron Smith and *Aethlon: The Journal of Sports Literature* for previously publishing these five poems (20180107, 20180109, 20180114, 20180117, and 20180320) as "I'm Not Driving" in Issue XXXVI:1 Fall 2018/Winter 2019.

Thank you to Susumu Takiguchi for previously publishing these five haibun (20180313, 20180324, 20180326, 20180711, and 20181212) in the Autumn 2020 edition of *World Haiku Review*.

Publisher: Leah Huete de Maines
Editor: Christen Kincaid
Cover Art: Eric Chandler
Author Photo: Eric Chandler (Image: Leo at Parent Lake along Kekekabic Trail.)
Cover Design: Elizabeth Maines McCleavy

Order online: www.finishinglinepress.com
also available on amazon.com

Author inquiries and mail orders:
Finishing Line Press
P. O. Box 1626
Georgetown, Kentucky 40324
U. S. A.

Table of Contents

To Stephen and Natalie Chandler
who taught me to move around and pay attention.

Introduction

In 2018, I wrote a poem after every workout. I put down my thoughts after every cross-country ski trip. After every run, hike, or paddle. A few months into this project, I remembered the haibun with its combination of prose and haiku. I stuck with that form for the rest of the year. It seemed like a good way to pay attention to the world, both at home in Duluth, Minnesota and while on the road as an airline pilot. When the year ended, I stopped writing haibun. But this project had a lasting impact on me. I keep paying close attention when I'm out moving around, even though I don't write a daily poem anymore.

I was curious about the form itself. Late in 2019, I read *The Essential Bashō* by Matsuo Bashō (Translated by Sam Hamill). Why not learn about haibun by reading work by the man who invented the form? Matsuo Bashō was a famous 17th Century Japanese poet. He used haibun as a travelogue during long journeys on foot through Honshu, the main island of Japan. In his most famous collection, *Narrow Road to the Interior*, Bashō wrote haibun during a 1200-mile, 5-month-long trip he took on foot. In 2018, I took one of the most adventurous, solo backpacking trips of my life. My dog Leo and I hiked for five days through the Boundary Waters Canoe Area Wilderness of Minnesota. We followed the Kekekabic Trail. I wrote haibun during that trip and throughout the year. By accident, I stumbled on a form that Bashō used the same way: As a log of his journeys. The hiking similarity was almost spooky.

Purists might find fault with my attempts at haibun. I studied several definitions of the form and my work may fall short. In Bashō's collection *The Knapsack Notebook*, he wrote a haibun about falling off a horse in a mountain pass. He critiqued his own haiku there by saying, "I note the absence of a seasonal word." But it didn't stop him from publishing it. In Hamill's translation, he writes that Bashō said, "Abide by rules, then throw them out!—only then may you achieve true freedom." I did it backwards. I threw the rules out, then tried to learn them afterwards.

I followed the intent of Bashō's haibun form, though. Hamill comments that Bashō "believed that poetry should arise naturally from close observation, revealing itself in the careful use of ordinary language." I wasn't just jogging. I was trying to pay attention. To carve out meaning. In *The Knapsack Notebook*, Bashō said, "Nothing's worth noting that is not seen with fresh eyes. You will find in my notebook random observations from along the road, experiences and images that linger in heart and mind…"

I saw little things. I heard snippets of conversation. Sometimes while hiking in the wilderness, sometimes while running through some hard neighborhoods. Bashō said, "People often say that the greatest pleasures of traveling are finding a sage hidden behind the weeds or treasures hidden in trash, gold among discarded pottery."

It's a loss if skiing through the woods is just a workout. All these miles moving over the earth under my own power have meaning. These haibun help me find more.

Prologue

20180107
Chicago treadmill
Run
5.5 miles

I was supposed to run six miles.
I listened to a
Benedictine monk
talk about spirituality.
He said that,
Anything that lifts your heart is a prayer.
If fishing is what lifts your heart, then
fishing is a prayer.

At 5.5 miles the phone rang.
The basement in our new house is flooding.

Apparently, I don't have to show gratitude for this.
But I am supposed to seek the opportunity presented here
and
avail
myself of it.

20180109
Jamaica treadmill
Run
4 miles

Torrential rain
forces me inside.
I feel like the opposite of a fish tank.
I'm inside the glass,
but the water's outside.

And just before bed,
I will learn that there's a tsunami warning.
The one time I layover in the Caribbean.

20180114
Duluth
Cross-Country Ski
10k

We got home
and my son
apologized for being distracted
while we were skiing.

I laughed.

All I remembered
was us silently moving
through the trees.

I think
at single-digit temperatures
the temperature stands for
how many fingers
won't freeze.

20180117
Phoenix treadmill
Run
6 miles

sore back
from shoveling
so much snow
so many times
but I can still run

doesn't hurt at all
when I run

20180313
Duluth
Run
5.2 miles

    How many days in a row has the sun risen into a clear blue sky? The streak's getting pretty long. The wind stacked the pack ice up at the *fond du lac*. The yellow sun sends a yellow stripe across the open water and it hits the shelf of ice and disperses. Brilliant sparkles randomly dot the expanse as the shards reflect the sun. My legs are rusty.

    The grass and mud are
    exposed. But they are not free.
    Winter still holds on.

20180317
Duluth
Run
12 miles

    While I procrastinated by binge watching something on Netflix, I saw the shadow of a bird outside the door to the basement. I was mildly curious, but went back to watching the show. Then it happened again and my curiosity got to me. I lifted the shade to find that a chickadee was stuck between the storm door and the house door. We had some wonky old doorknobs that have a strange locking mechanism, so Shelley took them out of the door completely. Chickadee must've gotten in through the doorknob hole. I opened the door, opened the outer door and the chickadee flew away with his little black cap. I put on my shoes and escaped myself down the shore road next to all the pancake ice on a beautiful, calm sunny day.

    I saw the two bears
    climb from the icy culvert.
    Dazzled by the sun.

20180320
Orlando treadmill
Run
4 miles

When I'm on the treadmill
My phone thinks I'm driving.
I'm not driving.
It gives me credit
for moving across the land but
I'm not driving.
I click on the button for the lawyers.
I'm not likely to crash
on the treadmill because
I'm not driving.
But I am telling the truth.
I'm not driving.
I'm not driving.
I'm not.

20180321
Vancouver
Run
8.4 miles

  I run through the science fiction apartment buildings. A city skyline that I don't recognize that looks clean and inviting. Floatplanes come and go at the seaplane base. I run past Aerodynamic Forms in Space. The rowing club. Along the seawall past the sprinter statue. The 9 o'clock gun. The Brockton Light. The Girl in a Swimsuit. Snow marbles the green-blue mountainsides across the bay of blue-green water. I pass under the Lions Gate, green and vertical. Around the bend and into the sun, the Pacific Ocean stretches out. Holds ten ships, stacked up at anchor. The Siwash Rock a sentinel guarding the strait. I'm running faster than I deserve to. I transect the park on the Tatlow Trail, tiny next to the towering trees.

  The tree on the rock
  doesn't mind all the people.
  I wish I didn't.

20180324
Duluth
Run
12.7 miles

  This is the spring that you forget exists. You come out of winter and feel like forty degrees is the heart of summer. Then you readjust. And the same forty degrees feels cold. And the wind blows over the lake from the east. And the skies fill with overcast. And you know you have to put on winter gear for your long run. But you're smart, so you head off up the Old Shore Road, the extension of Superior Street to the east. It's been repaved. Smooth and isolated. I think I saw one car. Go into the teeth of the wind first so that you're like a sail on the way home.

  It's a long run so
  you put the wind at your back
  at the turn and fly.

20180325
Duluth
Cross-Country Ski
7.2k

John said I could take Leo anywhere. If you must have zero paw prints for your Olympic training program, you have over 100 other miles of ski trails inside a 20-mile ring. Go there. Leave Snowflake to the dogs. John figures there's a week of skiing left. Amazing how you leave the dry roads and brown ditches behind. When we get into the trail, it's as good as it gets. Deep snow and blue sky, freshly groomed. Leo seemed happy. I did Special K one extra loop at the end. I set my PR according to the satellites. Still kicking at age 50 here at the far end of the season. Probably the last time of the year for me and my ski buddy.

He rolls on his back.
Can he feel joy? Or maybe
he's just got an itch.

20180326
Duluth
Run
4.3 miles

      Leo gets weird when we go for a run on the Lakewalk. He seems to think of it as a chore to be on a leash on the pavement. He hangs back all the way out and pulls hard to get home. I try to give him as much time as I can off the leash. We always head down from that first park bench after exiting under the railroad tunnel by the Holiday Station. We go down to the Endion Ledges. They're exposed now. He runs free for a little bit on the rocks. Rolls on his back. His signature move. Then I tie him up again as we go in front of the fancy townhomes. We run past Scott Anderson's plaque until the satellites say I've gone at least far enough to get a four-miler out of the turnaround. Leo knows we're headed back and pulls ahead. He fully expresses himself. There is no deceit.

      The ledges are out.
      The ice blurs the line between
      the lake and the shore.

20180330
Houston treadmill yesterday
San Juan, Puerto Rico treadmill today
Run
2.5 miles

Looking out the window of the hotel at a Maxfield Parrish painting of clouds over the ocean north of Puerto Rico. Yesterday, I felt an overwhelming sense of loss because during my trips to the war, I didn't spend every spare minute taking notes. I took notes. I wrote emails. I wrote stick-figure-theater letters to my kids. But I was pretty task saturated and didn't have the snot left at the end of the day to write. I should have. I worked out and read. I should've worked out and written. I could hear the birds outside in the springtime green trees outside the Houston Marriott, stuck in the middle of the airport like Tom Hanks.

But today, as I looked at the beach and the crashing waves over the video screen on the treadmill, I listened to Naomi Shihab Nye say that I didn't have to spend my whole life on a big project. I could write three sentences a day and that would be enough to start connecting things together. To start seeing things. So, I felt better. This strange attempt to write surrounding each day of running/skiing/etc. seems more worthwhile now. They say the best time to plant a tree is 20 years ago. And the next best time to plant one is right now.

I stood on the beach
wearing jeans and a t-shirt.
It's snowing at home.

20180421
Duluth
Run
16 miles

      I don't like running on the road. I prefer trails. But I have to as part of my self-imposed plan. I saw a rabbit and a deer eating my yard while I grabbed my GPS watch out of the charger. I saw five geese fly north over me while I headed into the sun along the Lakewalk. I saw fishing boats zig-zagging through the open water on Lake Superior off Brighton Beach. I started running at 7:30 am, but somehow, the sun seems like it's high. High enough that there isn't the line of a reflection across the water like there is at dawn. So, there were vast areas of the surface of the lake, some like a mirror, some opaque. Hard to say which was ice and which was water. Finally saw some waterfowl land on the same texture as where the fishing boats motored. I don't like running on the road. But, if you must, several hours near Lake Superior will do.

      Is the surface of
      the big lake ice or water?
      The answer is yes.

20180606
Chicago treadmill
Run
3 miles

When I was at Camp Losano, the Air Force hooches at Kandahar AB in Afghanistan, I used to go run in the gym pretty often. It was only a few steps away from our conex apartments. I'd go in there, get on a treadmill and go. Often, I was still all fired up from go-pills so got a lot of good running in. No way in hell I was going to run outside at Kandahar. Probably get run over by an MRAP or a Toyota HiLux.

I'd run next to the roaring tube providing air-conditioned air. I'd think of Duluth and imagine I was running along the Superior Hiking Trail through Duluth, up high, looking over the lake.

Today, I was in Chicago, staring at a flat, opaque film of glass that separates the treadmill from the swimming pool. I thought about Duluth again. Maybe I'm just rationalizing the dreadmill run. But it can still be worthwhile. Who's to say what I imagine isn't as nice as the real thing? I run and imagine, even while listening to a podcast.

> I can imagine
> the trail, the lake, and the sun.
> Who's to say what's real?

20180609
Chicago treadmill
Run
7 miles

This was the last long run before Grandma's. I listened to a New Yorker Poetry podcast about "groping for the portal" where the words can be released. It made sense somehow. Also a Zen monk talked about what makes us all human. Seems futile.

I found myself thinking about the rhubarb plants. I planted two before this three-day trip started. One with a penny that said 2017 (the one closest to the steps) and another with a penny that said 2001 (since 2001 is what brought us to Duluth). My dad said something about planting a penny with that year's date on it with the rhubarb. Some sort of ritual. I'll google it later and see if it's real.

This morning, Shelley texted me about the "fucking deer." I asked if they ate my rhubarb plants. She said they did. I said really? and she said no. I got pranked about my rhubarbs. I didn't think it was funny.

> I keep having firsts.
> I'm too old to learn what a
> wild cherry looks like.

20180610
Toronto
Run
5.2 miles

I ran to Coronation Park. I was reminded, under the giant Canadian flag, that they were our ally during WWII. There was a memorial that said Canada had 11 million people. One million of them enlisted to help in the war.

I ran back past the dog park, along the bicycle path, beside the light rail line, by the Music Park. Under the giant CN phallus. As I passed the marina, there was a Canada goose floating in the water.

The waterfowl swims.
In Canada, they just call
this big bird a goose.

20180611
Sacramento
Run
4 miles

    I went out into the heat and ran down the sidewalk under the Sewing Machine sign that marked a closed repair shop but there was a homeless guy underneath with skin so brown it was almost black from the sun and I kept going over the train tracks so modern and shiny and over the black spots from the spat out gum and past the guy in the tunnel who was busking playing drums and as I came out of the tunnel a police car drove down into what was a pedestrian way, I thought, and when I came back later there was no drummer, to the river past the touristy shops and Old Sacramento and downstream the Sacramento River when I normally go upstream. More homeless people. So hot in the pavement sun along the railroad tracks.

    I normally go
upstream, but I wanted to
follow the river.

20180711
Toronto
Run
4.7 miles

For a change, I ran down York and when I got to the waterfront I turned to the left. To the East. I dodged pedestrians and found my way out to a park that was a long tunnel of shade made by maple trees. The cobblestones and pavers had big shapes of maple leaves under the trees themselves. I ran through the tunnel and along the water of Lake Ontario. There was a sailing regatta, blistering white in the afternoon sun. A lot like Duluth in that it's a working waterfront. Grain elevators. Cranes and derricks. I followed a path made for bikes into the harsh light and returned along the same path, into the shade of the maples. It's Canada after all.

And along a brook, as I returned to the maples, there was a poem hanging on a tree. Well, it was more like a motivational statement, but still weird enough to be cool.

The leaves gave me shade
with unique palmately veined
blades. I like maples.

20180718
Salt Lake City
Run
6.7 miles

All those seven years we lived in Utah, I never made it up to the capitol building. So, as I ran uphill (walked by this point) I realized it's never too late to come up with a first. The 96F heat was brutal but somehow tolerable at the same time. Dry. Bouts of shade. I kept striding uphill, almost ski-walking, and finally they deigned to make a sidewalk. I walked through the manicured tiny patches of irrigated grass and suddenly found myself in front of a vacant lot. A half-full 40. Lots of broken glass. A beat-to-hell vacant lot with an amazing view of Salt Lake City and the airport. And then another million dollar house. A covey of quail bizarrely strutted alongside me. A lizard. I hoped I wouldn't step on a rattlesnake. No more shade as I followed the trail to the top of Ensign Peak. I got to the top, like Brigham Young. This was the place, indeed. Antelope Island, over the city and to the sweep of Little and Big Cottonwood and Mill Creek Canyon where we got married. And then downhill through the heat boiling up from the pavement.

I run by the spires
of the temple until I
find my holy place.

20180721
Whiteface Reservoir
Paddleboard
1.9 miles

      Just the day after I forgot our anniversary, I took her paddleboard across to the marsh, chasing the shriek of the bald eagles somewhere across. In the bog/marsh, it sat in a dead tree and watched me walk on water. On the water that you can't see down into. Black. Like tea when some of it washed up onto the board over my toes as I paddled. But in the deep, black and impenetrable.

      Like morning coffee
      the lake is also like black
      medicine water.

20180722
Whiteface Reservoir
Kayak
4 miles

      I drag the 20-year-old white plastic kayak down the railroad-tie steps before everyone's awake. A loon. A bald eagle. A mom and some little kids and a dog out on a dock. A beaver lodge. Another bald eagle. Maybe the same one. An island, the one with the geocache on it. The one with the tiny cove, just big enough to fit the kayak into. Surrounded by a red pine amphitheater. I'd be okay of some of my ashes were placed here in the winter.

      When I'm all burned up,
      I'd be fine with being like
      Paddle to the Sea.

20180727
Portland, Oregon
Run
7.2 miles

    Smarter finding the way through the city streets of Portland this time. Up the steep street to Washington Park and past the Lewis and Clark monument to Sacajawea and Jean Baptiste. She pointed up past the construction, coaching me to get some more uphill trail miles. I found the MAC trail and ran along the trail, past the archery range where a class was setting up to loose their arrows. I found the Wildwood trail and the giant trees and ferns and green undergrowth and vines looked like Endor. Some hikers came by with their dogs. Even a Goth hiker all dressed in black. Found the turnaround and think I saw Mt. Adams in the hazy distance. A beautiful, sunny morning trail run. I retraced my steps, took a new branch of the Wildwood trail down past the Japanese garden into the busy parking lot, lines of people squinting at the instructions at the pay stations, but all looking eager to spend time in the morning sun. A Friday, but felt like a Saturday as I ran past them to the steps that opened onto the center of the rose test garden. Stunning in the sun.

    I pounded down the hill to the hotel, refreshed.

I think more people
should go outside. I think they'd
be much happier.

20180729
Fort Worth
Run
4.2 miles

      So hot that I had to walk. But at the turnaround, there was a duck with her ducklings. And an egret. As the water burbled over the low-head dam.

      It looked like a fish
      but ripples in the water
      were from a turtle.

20180730
Duluth (Tischer/Bagley/Hartley)
Run
7.2 miles

Just started doing this run a few years ago. It's hard to believe how lush and green the trails are when the lawns are starting to dry up. I stopped at the top of the hill in Hartley and had a juneberry. It had gone by, but it was still tasty. Hot out, but not in the shade. First time wearing the trail shoes in a while. They felt good.

> The long green tunnel
> makes it easier to run
> away from the sun.

20180801
Duluth
Run
5.7 miles

Hard to believe that too hot can turn into too cold here in Duluth overnight. The 50 degree temps and the spitting rain.

How can you go from
sunscreen and sunglasses to
a winter jacket?

20180803
Duluth
Run
7.5 miles

It's the same route as July 30th. Just backwards. Past the Little League game. Past the church. Connecting to the Superior Hiking Trail into Hartley. Past the Nature Center. The rolling trail up into the ski trails. Past the juneberries of the other day. Trail familiar, yet somehow not, simply by running it the other direction. New perspective. Down and down and down the Tischer Creek. Almost masked by a city, but I mark her path with my feet. Down and down to my house.

> Let us now praise the
> famous creek that flows past the
> beaver's home to mine.

20180806
Austin, Texas
Run
5.1 miles

    We descended through the popcorn clouds into Texas. The temperature is around 80F, so it shouldn't be TOO, too bad. But it is. Spend a little time talking to Becker about nothing until you're almost frost-bitten in the hotel room. Then you step out into the sun and it's like lava. Dramatically, different in the shade. More dramatic than in Salt Lake City the other day. Starting from the hotel near O. Henry's house down to Lady Bird Lake. Along the river, under the place where the bats will come out. I think I could hear them squeaking as I ran over the new pedestrian walkway under the bridge. Nice. Lots of dogs out for walks, cooling off in the lake/river. I ran by Stevie Ray Vaughan's statue. Somebody placed flowers in his right hand. I went up Barton Creek for a change. Paddleboards, canoes, a public pool. And somehow the smell like I stepped in dog crap. I stopped to check my shoes. Clean. So hot, on the way back over a pedestrian bridge, I gave up trying. Walked, staggered in the heat.

    Shade provides comfort
    for the bats, maybe, but not
    for the Duluth man.

20180905
Kekekabic Trail (Day 1)
Hike
5.4 miles

Yesterday dropped Toyota at east end (308 miles round trip) and today, Shelley took me to Ely on the west end (about 200 round trip for her.) Got to the US Forest Service office east of town and got my permit. Got to the trailhead and gave up about 5 pounds of stuff. Weighed in at 60 pounds at home. Seemed too much so dropped Keens, collapsible dog bowl, tarp (ground cloth), and some other odds and ends. Crystal clear all day. Buggy (mosquitoes) towards end. Landmarks like guidebook says. Lots of brushwork, clearing fallen trees. Leo stayed pretty close. Pack felt okay. Took one slip in a little chimney-like part of the trail and scraped my right forearm. Actually had cell service before turning to Parent Lake campsite. Sent a few texts. Also used Spot GPS unit to say ok at site and "setting up for the night." Biolite solar panel working well (re-charge of phone). 5.4 miles in 3.5 hours. About 1.5 mph. Saw another canoe here, northeast corner of the lake. Seagulls. Eagle or osprey over tent. Couldn't find latrine? Several beaver dams, not fresh. Chased many chipmunks and treed one and barked some. Water filter works quicker than I remembered. Veggie chili, granola bar, apple cider. Maybe binoculars next time? Just can't believe I have a 55 pound pack.

Shelley seemed nervous. I was too. This is bigger than I've done in a while. Just watch each step and take your time. The hardest part is getting the pack on. Once it's on it's not too bad. Glad I brought Shelley's classic cross-country ski poles (135cm). They've been very helpful, especially with tricky footing and downhills. Miss the kids and sorry to not see Thursday and Friday cross-country races.

Sun is setting. Wind dying down like it somehow manages to do each night. Blowing little ankle slappers into the shore. Evergreen with sharp, white poplars along the blue water's edge. Not a single cloud. And from the moment we hit the woods, it smelled like they do in the fall. The green leaves look tired. A few have turned and fallen. Asters.
Leo keeps looking at me like, "So, now we go back to the truck, right?"

Just like an airline
trip, I said. Except this is
a comm-out gameplan.

20180906
Kekekabic Trail (Day 2)
Hike
6.6 miles

In the tent for 11 hours. Lots of loons. Huge squirrels and sounds kept me up. Leo snored all night. Next site to northeast along Parent Lake talked (shouted) until 4 am. Jet noise.

> The loons wail at night.
> The airliner flies over
> and joins the chorus.

From Snowbank Lake Trail intersection for about 3 miles to the east were many newer blowdowns. Spent dozens of times on all fours and dozens crawling over and around. Last 3 miles was just brushy which was a blessing. Skinned my knees. Kind of wish I wore pants instead of shorts. Ski poles are huge help going over blowdowns and uphill. Saw bandsaw blade and lunched at Drumstick Lake. Leo and I were both getting thirsty. Still have mobile phone sometimes. Relief to get to Medas Lake. Hot. Went swimming. Dried boots and socks and wet underwear. Filtered water. Ceramic filter gumming up. Grace had a good race via text. SPOT GPS is working. Saw bush plane and airliners. So much for quietest in the country, Backpacker Magazine. At least there may be no people shouting.

> A scraggly jack pine
> keeps the rock ledge from sliding
> down into the lake.

20180907
Kekekabic Trail (Day 3)
Hike
12.4 miles

Tail-slapping beavers sounded like full-grown men jumping into the lake. Other than that, pretty good sleep. Thomas Lake portage was pretty. Single log bridge. Met Willy and Reggy from Switzerland! They were portaging down from a 15-day trip. They worked for Dow in Michigan and did their first trip in the 70's and come back regular. Leo behaved. They had bear spray if he didn't. Willy offered me a can. I turned it down. Hope I don't regret it. Portage trails are crazy nice compared to the Kek. Tiny maples along ridge by Mosquito Lake. Good walking to Strup Lake and report said it was cleared to Harness, so off we went. Super-hot near 2011 burn as we climb in sun. Eerie burned out trees. Nice view of Bakekana Lake. Hard climb to Kek mountain spur. Misjudged water so stopped in a bog at the foot of the hill to refill. Short sharp hills to Harness Lake. No real spots. Tent is basically on trail. Couldn't find latrine. No place to hang bear bag, so I'm putting it over by smelly fire grate away from us. Half-assed job of it in a pine but oh well.

Today's hike was hard.
The body is holding up.
Thanks, Ibuprofen.

20180908
Kekekabic Trail (Day 4)
Hike
7 miles

Can't imagine the last 3 of this day being the end of a 12-mile day. Glad I did the long day yesterday. 3 grouse on the trail early. Geese flew at us over breakfast. Back a little twitchy, so took 800 mg of Ibuprofen. They oversold the high point as having views. I could feel the Twin Peaks and could see the eastern one from a lookout on high point, but only took one photo because I was waiting for the "rocky outcrop." Lots of moose nuggets. Going up to high point very brushy, as advertised. Good easy walking into Agamok River. Very pretty falls. Leo and I napped and hydrated. I took 800 mg more of Motrin. Now, after supper, my stomach has me feeling a little nauseous. Motrin? Bad water? Dehydrated? I think the Motrin. Also, at breakfast, learned I had to grill the powdered eggs. Will need to do same tomorrow. Portage trails are like autobahn compared to the Kek.

Also, per book, reroute had to follow through Cavity Lake fire area east of Agamok. Got lost for 30 minutes. Exhausting bushwhack, but gameplan to rejoin trail worked. (Lost 6 more times, only briefly) Hot sun at the time didn't help. Surreal 12-year-old poplar forest with burned trunks sticking up. Gabimichigami site barely big enough. Has latrine though. Hard to find place to hang bear bag again. They weren't kidding about getting lost. Very brushy. I'm worried about 10 mile day tomorrow if it's the same.

Dad, I think we're lost.
"You're only lost if you don't
know what to do next."

20180909
Kekekabic Trail (Day 5)
Hike
10 miles

On the last day I had ten more miles to go. It should've been pretty manageable. But the first 9 miles was a slog. Again. Lots of brush. Wolf scat at my feet not long after we started. Black and shiny and a huge pile, fresh but not steaming. It's the way of things: Keeps getting tougher right until the end. A second pile of wolf scat. At least I remembered to take a picture this time. Agitated. Not hungry. Semi-nauseous for three days now. I think in ketosis. Bingoshick Lake. A weird cedar stand. Beautiful. Before this we stopped early on Seahorse Lake for a break. Can't seem to drink enough water. Somehow dehydrated after quarts and quarts. Windy as we sat on the east end of Bingoshick. 3 miles to go. A young grouse on a beaver path. Leo finally saw him. Clucking like a chicken gave him away. Mine Lake was high so a half mile of bushwhacking just ten feet to the side of the trail. Rarely so happy to see cleared trail with one mile to go. Past the BWCA sign, the Paulson Mine, the tree fungus with "Luv from MN" (smiley face) drawn on it. My truck. Big relief. Gas station. Milk bones. Relief. Leo pukes grass in back seat. DQ burger was the best in the world.

> The sound of peace is
> my dog snoring on a rock
> on a wild lakeshore.

20181001
Kansas City
Run
3.4 miles

I haven't run in a long while. Hotel layover for the first time since early August and the habits of my hotel life takeover. At first, I don't recognize the hotel. After I went running and went to the mezzanine restaurant for the ease, convenience, and airline discount, I recognized the bar as a place I went once before. Just as loud this time with a Chiefs game on the big screen. The run, through stop lights and lights of red hands. Up the steps to the World War One Memorial, dedicated in 1921 by Pershing and Foch. A tower, a museum underground, art of poppies at the entrance signifying the dead. Naturally the museum is closed on Mondays. I ran past another statue called The Hiker, memorializing those who fought in the Spanish American War in Cuba and the Philippines and the Boxer Rebellion. Another memorial that mentioned a Tree, planted for the Marine war dead of World War Two. A lot of memorials, made after the wars ended, but not so far after that they felt like war was something that would go on forever. Remembering the dead and maybe thinking that war was over. Thinking it was a bug and not a feature.

The sphinx named "Future"
hides its face so it won't have
to see the next war.

20181009
Fort Lauderdale
Run
2.6 miles

I step out of the air conditioning and am actually cold as I hit the outside air. The sweet, sticky smell of the Atlantic. There's the disorienting period of time where I start to run, all the systems begin to run and I realize that it's actually far too hot for my Duluth blood. Ships anchored offshore. Down the sidewalk past the lifeguard stations. Out onto the beach where the ocean pushes up lines of seaweed. Plastic bottlecaps. Footprints. Exhaustion. A southeast wind here and over in the gulf, a hurricane.

I call the ships "salties."
But here at the ocean, what
else would you call them?

20181017
Duluth
Rollerski
8.7 miles

      Bright sun and fall foliage still hanging on along the Munger Trail. Joy and guilt, knowing should've been doing this all summer and this is the first time. Only a few other people out. but it is a work day after all. I used to start rolling on July 4th, but that was years ago in Alaska. Today, it was just me realizing that my hands haven't calloused up yet like they should and I have a long way to go. Fighting father time on the sweet new pavement out on the Munger.

      On the way back, a
      guy says there's a kingfisher
      sitting on the wire.

20181020
Duluth
Run
3.7 miles

Sunny but cold and breezy. The sun shining down and reflecting so hard off the water toward the lift bridge that it hurts. Running for just a half hour turns into more when we find a teddy bear on the ground partway home. We figure it's the person that had the stroller that we passed headed toward Leif Erikson park. So Sam tore off after them carrying a teddy bear into the sun. He won: He got more miles and it was their teddy bear.

It's fun to go run
into the sun and rescue
some little kid's bear.

20181021
Duluth
Rollerski
6.9 miles

      Lots of yellow poplar leaves all over the pavement as I followed the kids up the Munger Trail. Sun low and in our eyes even in the early afternoon. Lots of people out in the Munger Inn parking lot on this Sunday afternoon. We had to wait for the Lake Superior tourist train to pass before we could start. I double-poled out and the kids pulled away. Mama was sweep on her bike. We took a picture over the St. Louis River valley at the turnaround and I tried to keep up with the kids on the way back down. Rollerskiing is almost its own season. Its own sport. I enjoy it, even though it only exists as preparation for the real thing on snow. We figure it's the first time we've all three of us rollerskied together. Doesn't seem possible. Never too late for firsts, I guess.

      Roll toward the sun.
      Gold poplar leaves fill the trail.
      The wheels hum; poles click.

20181107
Vancouver
Run
5.2 miles

      50F is just about the coldest I like to run with just airline travel clothes. I wore my work t-shirt under my running t-shirt and still a bit chilly. But sunny and calm. I found the Robert Burns statue. And the Lord Stanley statue. I just learned today that this Stanley Park is indeed the same Stanley Park of Lord Stanley of the Stanley Cup. I have run here several times, enjoyed it a lot and never put the two together until today. I was in the cockpit over the Canadian Rockies and looking at Google maps. I saw that there was a Lord Stanley statue in the park as I daydreamed about my upcoming run. That's when it clicked. Lord Stanley's Cup. Son of a gun. Beautiful trees, monster tree along the road, ran by Beaver Lake for the first time. Seawall by Siwash Rock under construction, but very nice. And saw the three trees and some markers at the Air Force Garden of Remembrance along the trail in the woods. Quite a spot, this Stanley Park.

      Down over the hills
      and landing so I can go
      run up some others.

20181113
Salt Lake City
Run
7.6 miles

The sun seemed low in the sky. Not much time left. Just above 40F but the sun makes it seem like its warmer. I leave the work t-shirt under my running t-shirt and head uphill past the temple and the tabernacle. Up the winding creek into the park. Up up up the road. The valley in shadow. Lots of dogs, which is nice. The yellow sunlight lights up the eastern wall of the canyon. I find the Bonneville Shoreline Trailhead. But I stay on the pavement and find ice in a seep of water across the pavement. I'm cold. I head downhill. My Garmin battery freezes. I feel good, but cold. 39F on the bank sign when I get back in the dark.

Reminded of the days when on layovers in 2001 and Shelley would bring Sam down to the city from South Ogden and we'd walk his stroller up the same road.

I never made it
so far up the creek before.
No paddle either.

20181129
San Diego
Run
6.6 miles

I ran to Harbor Island from the Westin. I was in a bad mood. By the west end of the island, I saw two pelicans floating by the rocks surrounded by a bunch of jeering seagulls. A kid leaned out of the open car window and simply smiled and waved his hand. I felt better.

A lady saw my Grandma's marathon shirt as I was waiting for a crosswalk.

"Grandma's?! That's my favorite!"

Without even realizing it, I flashed her a shaka sign with my hand and smiled.

The strange part is that
a person helped my mood by
looking at my shirt.

20181211
Fort Lauderdale
Run
3.4 miles

  How can it be chilly? People wearing full on winter coats and hats. Me in shorts and a t-shirt. Around the corner and out to the shore road. That crisp thread between the light blue of the sky and the dark blue of the water. Strong wind out of the northwest, a salty anchored offshore. Along the red square bricks, laid diagonally. Past the cigarette smokers. Past the marijuana smokers. Past the guy lifting dumbbells while he stands at the seawall, looking at the ocean while his car speakers thump. Lots of battery operated scooters going too fast and too close. A truck with giant pipe peels out from a stoplight.

  I went down to the water. I got a moment's peace and then found my way back to my room through the noise.

  The waves hit the beach
  and the highest reach of the
  foam moves north to south.

20181212
Albuquerque
Run
5.5 miles

Highs and lows. Googled a town I haven't been in since 1990 or so. Found my way to the Rio Grande. Stood there after plunging through the cottonwoods. Canada geese paddled across the river. Past some ponds on the path. Ducks and waterfowl in the high desert. Weird. Some local kids on mountain bikes as I got closer to the old Highway 66. Novices smiling. Bosque Youth Conservation Corps sign. I was happy. Ran down the busy street to Old Albuquerque. San Felipe de Neri church. "Guarded" by two replica Confederate cannons from the Civil War. Buried near the church so the Union wouldn't get them. Guy who buried them came back to unbury them after the war. Not sure what the point was. Guy playing a pan flute near the plaza of the old city. Nearly killed by a woman pulling out of a parking lot. Huge black SUV and the woman shouting "sorry sorry sorry" at my back as I ran down the sidewalk from dodging her into the street.

Small adventures are
for me. I ran on the banks
of the Rio Grande.

20181220
Fort Lauderdale
Run
4.4 miles

      The wind was roaring out of the south, so I went into the wind first. The road bent away from the beach, so I decided to run along the water. Sandblasted and watching dunes form in front of my eyes. Then a ship's horn, reminding me of the captain's salute as a boat toots at the lift bridge. Then the massive cruise ship appeared moving sideways from the right to the left. I found my way back to A1A. Past the boots and cats and boots and cats music coming out of the bars. Dodging the electric scooters. Downwind now, I was struck that the world of man and the world of nature kind of reach toward one another at the border. The palm trees grow out of the sidewalk and the beach chairs cover the sand. Nature reaching toward man and man reaching toward nature. Like one of the wood carvings by Escher. Night vs. Day. Sky vs. Water. The border not distinct but blurred.

      The ship was so big.
      Like a piece of the city
      was floating away.

20181230
Korkki Nordic Center
Cross-Country Ski
10.4k

      I don't imagine Grace thinks about the fact that Korkki was where she took her first strides on skis. I think about it every time. All the time. It was a day where all the trees are flocked in white. We stopped for a few pictures. We didn't say much. I felt like my heart would explode due to an overload of blue kick wax joy, gliding through the trees in the silence. We got back to the cabin and warmed up. I told her it was one of the best skis of my whole life. She looked confused.

      Two human beings
      moving across the cold snow.
      Why does this please me?

Epilogue

20190228
Anaheim
Run
6.2 miles

Heron and a fish.
The ancient duel right there
in an LA ditch.

About the Author

Eric Chandler is the author of *Hugging This Rock: Poems of Earth & Sky, Love & War* (Middle West Press, 2017). His writing has appeared in *Northern Wilds, Grey Sparrow Journal, The Talking Stick, Sleet Magazine, O-Dark-Thirty, Line of Advance, Collateral, The Deadly Writers Patrol, PANK, The Wrath-Bearing Tree,* and *Columbia Journal.* Chandler was nominated for a Pushcart Prize in 2014 for creative nonfiction. He's a three-time winner of the Col. Darron L. Wright Award for poetry. He's a member of Lake Superior Writers, the Outdoor Writers Association of America, and the Military Writers Guild.

Chandler is also a US Air Force veteran of both the active duty and the Minnesota Air National Guard. He flew 145 combat missions and over 3000 hours in the F-16. He deployed to Iraq three times for Operation Iraqi Freedom and once to Afghanistan for Operation Enduring Freedom. He retired as a lieutenant colonel in 2013.

Eric lives in Duluth, Minnesota where he cross-country skis as fast as he can. He's participated in both Grandma's Marathon in Duluth and the American Birkebeiner cross-country ski race in Wisconsin more times than he can remember. He's happiest when he's on a trail in the Arrowhead of Minnesota with his wife, two children, and faithful canine companion, Leo.